A Journal

CONTRACT ADMINISTRATION PITFALLS AND SOLUTIONS FOR ARCHITECT-ENGINEERING PROJECTS

Bob Jack

authorHOUSE®

AuthorHouse™
1663 Liberty Drive
Bloomington, IN 47403
www.authorhouse.com
Phone: 1 (800) 839-8640

Published by AuthorHouse 06/03/2015

ISBN: 978-1-5049-1560-1 (sc)
ISBN: 978-1-5049-1574-8 (e)

Print information available on the last page.

Any people depicted in stock imagery provided by Thinkstock are models, and such images are being used for illustrative purposes only. Certain stock imagery © Thinkstock.

This book is printed on acid-free paper.

Contents

Dedication

This Journal is dedicated to Jesse V. Harmon, a good friend and fellow contracts professional who was devoted to his profession and the people who practiced it.

Acknowledgements

I would like to express my thanks and appreciation to Christopher W. Larsen, AIA, and Gary L. Stone, Esq., for their advice and assistance in developing the content of this Journal.

About the Author

The author is William R.(Bob) Jack.

Bob is a native Californian, born January 4, 1941 in Santa Monica, California.

Bob is married and lives in North Las Vegas, Nevada with his wife Jane.

He has two surviving children by his first marriage. James, who lives in Southern California with his wife Nery, and two children Chris and Niki and his daughter, also Niki who lives in Wyoming with her husband Dave, with two children, Zach and Rick.

Bob grew up in Southern California in the San Gabriel Valley area not far from Los Angeles. Bob's youngest son Chris was killed in a pedestrian accident in Bakersfield,California at age 23 in 1997.

Bob graduated from Citrus High School, and Citrus College in Glendora,California and received his BA Degree in Economics from California State University at Los Angeles. He later went on to earn an MBA Degree from Azusa Pacific University and a Master of Science Degree in Advanced Management from Claremont Graduate University's Drucker School.

Bob's career spanned 40 years in various management postions in the aerospace, petroleum, academic research, nuclear energy and engineering fields. He spent the last 24 years of his career at a global engineering and construction company in Pasadena, California.

He is presently retired and spends his time traveling and writing. Bob's political works are frequently published in The Washington Times and

Las Vegas Sun, and are also published in the NY Times, Wall Street Journal and the LA Times.

Bob has authored three books. One about his son Chris named A Night in Darkness: The Drug Addicted Child. A second titled Living Within Yourself and this Journal. His next book will be published in the near future and will be titled A View from the Eagle's Nest: Policy Assessments During the Obama Era.

Foreword

Chapter 1 covers some of the most critical areas and frequent occurrences of defective contract administration, and describes solutions to these generally troublesome non- compliance issues, how they arise and time tested actions to prevent or resolve them.

In Chapter 2 is described the important things to consider in the Pre-Contract, Proposal and Negotiation phases of the project

Chapter 3 addresses the Contract Review and Execution (contract signing) phase, including the important contract tasks that must be addressed in this phase.

Chapter 4 covers the Project Initiation Phase, and the process by which it is implemented during the project.

Chapter 5 describes the important contract administration tasks during the Project Performance Phase and Chapter 6 covers the tasks that must be undertaken to close out the project.

Chapter 7 is the Summary and Conclusion of this Journal.

Chapter 1

Contract Administration Pitfalls and Solutions for Architect-Engineering Company

Companies of all sizes that are organized around customer funded projects are exposed to many challenges in performing their projects on time and within budget. Many of the pitfalls in performing such projects derive from inadequate contract administration. Effective contract administration is equally important to both customer and company. Sometimes work may be started and performed without a binding contract. This can result in liability exposures, and incurred costs that cannot be recovered. Often, the very people who are responsible for the direct performance of the work on the project are not familiar with the complete requirements of the contact for parts of the work they are charged with doing. This can result in serious performance problems, and the need for rework at the company's expense. The company may even become liable for impact costs which were reasonably foreseeable had the work been properly performed the first time. Other times staff departments, such as accounting are not knowledgeable of the way invoices are to be prepared for the contract. This results in billing and payment delays, and potentially disallowed costs. Audit provisions in the contract may expose the company to excessive examinations and years of records retention. The procurement staff may not be aware of the prime contract conditions that are to be incorporated into purchases made under the project or that prior customer approvals are required for purchases. This can result in compliance problems, and disallowed costs. The insurance staff may not be aware of special insurance requirements that fall outside the company's insurance policies, or of excessive liabilities that need to be insured. This can result in uninsured losses, and potentially, business threatening losses. The legal staff may not have reviewed the contract for special liability considerations, such as over reaching indemnification and warranty provisions and exposure to liability for consequential damages. The impacts can expose the company to costs, expenses, and liabilities that are entirely unnecessary and severely damaging. The project staff may perform additional services without a change in the compensation as provided for within the "Changes" clause of the contract, thereby reducing profit, exposing the company to additional risks and schedule overruns. These are but a few examples of the results and potential impacts from a firm's failure to put the proper emphasis on contract administration. A more detailed discussion of each of these areas will serve to illustrate the value of a strong emphasis on contract administration:

1. <u>Initiating work without a binding written contract.</u>

Beginning work without a binding written contract occurs more often than one might think. The customer may be in a hurry to get work started but may not yet have the final contract approved internally. Desiring to please the customer the company may open up a job number and begin work without yet having a written contract or notice to proceed (NTP). Various negative outcomes may occur if steps have not been taken to secure an adequate written NTP.

The NTP must be signed by a known authorized customer representative—someone who is an officer of the customer's organization, and who is familiar to the company's senior management. A job number should not be opened, or costs incurred, until an NTP is received. It's important to protect the company from potential lost costs that are incurred before the receipt and effective date of the NTP or fully executed contract.

If a contact has been negotiated, executed by the company and returned by the company for execution and the customer is willing to initiate the work via an NTP, the NTP should incorporate by reference or by physical attachment the terms of the final negotiated contract.

If the final contract has not been fully negotiated then the NTP should be worded such that the company is authorized to proceed with work *in accordance with its proposal to the customer*. This assumes that the proposal sufficiently detailed the basis of compensation, warranty, and limitations on the company's liabilities. If the proposal was not sufficient to cover these conditions then these must be incorporated in the NTP.

If these terms are not clear in the NTP when the company starts work, then the company's interests may be compromised (e.g. payments may not be received, and liabilities may include damages which the company has not excluded or limited). For architect-engineering contracts, the company would be liable at law for remediation of construction defects resulting from the company's services, in addition to remediation of its own A-E services.

If NTP compensation terms are not clear, the company may be limited to recovery of its direct costs, without allowance for gross profit.

Occasionally, the customer will issue a Letter Contract which authorizes the company to initiate and perform work under well defined terms and conditions. In effect, the Letter Contract is a formal contract that is merely issued as a prelude to a final and formal definitive contract. The Letter Contract is normally a contracting vehicle used by the Federal Government when the procuring agency is not able to secure all the internal agency approvals or meet all of the internal requirements in time for work to begin. Letter Contracts are limited in duration and funds, and the amounts incurred by the company before the formal definitive contract is received are called "pre contract costs." When the definitive contract is received there is a stipulation in the contract that all "pre contract costs" shall be treated in the same manner as though incurred under the definitive contract, and will be subject to the terms and conditions of the definitive contract.

The point is that any work performed by the company should be authorized in writing, and that this writing should contain terms that are in sufficient detail to ensure that the company will be paid for the work, and that it will not be exposed to any undue liabilities.

2. <u>Project technical staff being unfamiliar with detailed performance requirements.</u>

Contract assignments typically include a wide range of requirements that a number of persons within the company must perform or act on.

The Statement of Work must be carefully written to prevent excessive "Salesmanship" that exceeds the contract's actual requirements. For this reason it is essential that the project manager become thoroughly familiar with the obligations required under the contract, and that these obligations be distributed to and discussed with the persons who are actually going to have the responsibility for performing them.

Unfortunately, this does not always occur and the results are harmful to both the customer and the company. Especially today when company workers are spread throughout a large building, or may even share the work at different geographic locations it is very conceivable that a complete distribution of the contract requirements to all of those involved may be overlooked.

As discussed below, the Contract Administration Summary (CAS) is a tool that can be used to distribute the detailed contract requirements to various project participants, and is highly recommended for use by the A-E company. The CAS becomes a reliable document of record within the company, and one that can be used by all direct project and staff departments in the management and administration of the project.

3. <u>Accounting staff is not familiar with invoicing requirements.</u>

Because of the attention that must be given to the staffing and ramp up of the project, sometimes Accounting is delayed in its receipt of billing instructions and in invoicing the customer. The preparation of an accurate and complete invoicing instruction is something that requires a good deal of thought and in most A-E companies with a diverse customer base, these billing instructions vary widely from client to client.

Contracts that are cost reimbursable (CR) require the most attention by the billing section. In the negotiating phase of the contract attempts should be made to simplify the invoice support requirements needed for CR type contracts. This can be done by emphasizing that the customer (who has audit rights on CR type contracts) may rely on its audit rights to verify those costs which are invoiced, thereby significantly reducing the amount of invoice backup submitted. Accounting should review the proposed contract before negotiations, and comment on the billing provisions. These comments should be used during contract negotiations.

Invoice instructions must be thorough. These instructions may be part of the CAS or can be a separate piece of paper. For new customers normally it is a good practice for Accounting to prepare a prototype invoice at the beginning of the contract and submit it to the customer's paying office for review and approval. In this way, invoicing can start out on the right path.

The billing instruction should include the format for the invoice, customer name, customer address, job number identification information, the type of contract, basis for billing (progress payments for fixed price contracts, markups for CR type contracts), internal approvals needed for invoices prior to final issue, invoice support requirements, a copy of the invoicing and payment clause from the contract and any special instructions. Accounting should also be provided a copy of the entire contract for reference purposes.

Given that "cash flow" is critical to the typical firm providing professional services, it is impossible to overemphasize the importance of a thorough understanding of the compensation and billing requirements of the contract and preparing internal billing instructions that conform to contract requirements.

4. <u>Contact audit provisions may expose the company to excessive audit examinations and excessive years of records retention.</u>

Customers' standard audit clauses typically give the customer sweeping audit rights, and may sometimes not contain any limitation on the period of time that project records must be retained. These audits focus generally on two types of records—financial and nonfinancial. Financial audit rights affect the customers' rights to examine direct and indirect or overhead costs.

The audit rights clause should be reviewed by Accounting prior to negotiations. If the compensation provisions are for a commercial (non federal) fixed price contract, then there should be no financial audit rights given to the client. Contract rates should be negotiated for use in change orders (e.g. fixed "all in" labor rates by category, which include a fixed mark up with fringe costs, payroll expenses, overhead and profit, to be applied against any additional labor rate categories that may have been excluded, and a standard mark up % on other direct costs, where appropriate).

Where there is a direct cost reimbursable element to the contract, then audit rights should be limited to those direct costs elements. For example, in a Time and Materials (T&M) contract in which the labor rates are all inclusive fixed rates, but there are other direct costs (ODC) compensated on a straight cost reimbursable (CR) basis, audit rights should be limited the ODC and the quantity of labor hours expended (but no financial audit should be allowed of the fixed labor rate).

In some cases ODC items are charged at standard company commercial rates which are expressed on a rate schedule attached to the contract. These rates should not be subject to audit because they are commercial rates used on all company work, and can be compared by the customer to the rates charged for the same services on its other contracts, or what it can buy the services for in the private market. These standard rates include such items as reproduction and computer- aided design (CAD) usage.

As a general rule, financial audit rights by the customer should be limited under the contract to direct CR items, and direct charge units applied to the work, such as quantities of direct labor hours, or numbers of copies charged. No audit rights should be given to the client in any indirect/overhead accounts or in any fixed rates. All audit rights should be limited to the customer's *direct project account* in the company's books, and not extended to any other accounts in the company's books.

Where the project is with the Federal government, or is a subcontract under a federal prime contract, entirely different policies apply by federal mandate in the audit and records areas.

With regard to the examination of non financial records, these rights should also be limited to the project records compiled or relied on in the performance of work, such as calculations.

Finally, there should be a maximum time duration placed on the rights of the customer to access the records following final payment. It is suggested that one year be requested in negotiations (but never more than three years).

5. <u>The Procurement staff may not be aware of the prime contract conditions that are to be incorporated into purchase orders and subcontracts placed under the prime contract, or that prior customer approvals are required. This can lead to contract compliance and cost disallowance problems.</u>

The prime contract contains information and obligations which are to be placed into subcontracts. These are known as flow down provisions. Also, the prime contract usually provides that purchases and subcontracted services be approved in writing by the customer before they are awarded. There are also provisions that the company includes in these procurements to protect itself, such as audit, indemnity, warranty and insurance provisions. Those who perform the procurement function have a need to know the exact provisions and prior approval requirements of the prime contract in order to ensure that procurements are made in compliance with the terms of the prime contract.

There must be consistency between the terms of the prime contract and those of purchase orders and subcontracts placed under the prime contract. For example, where costs are auditable by the customer at the prime contract level, and are disallowed justifiably by the customer and some of these costs are the result of unallowable subcontract costs, the company must have the right to audit and, where necessary, recover these subcontract costs as well.

Also, where the warranty provisions of the prime contract require that defective prime contract work be re performed at no cost to the customer and some or all of this work has been performed by the subcontractor, the subcontract must contain a similar remedy for defective work, otherwise the company will be liable to the customer, but without recourse under the subcontract.

Another example of the need for prime contract and subcontract consistency involves indemnification. Where the company is required to defend, indemnify, and hold harmless the customer against and from injury or loss due to work performed under the prime contract, the company similarly wants to require that the subcontractor indemnify, defend and hold harmless not only the company, but also the customer against and from injury or loss for work performed under the subcontract.

Another area where there must be consistency between prime contract and the purchase orders and subcontracts issued under the prime contract is in regard to the statement of work. The work subcontracted and/or purchased items must fall exactly within the statement of work of the prime contract for the procurement costs to be allowable under the prime contract and for the purchased or subcontracted work to be consistent with the work authorized to be performed under the prime contract.

The above leads to the conclusion that procuring services and items from third parties under the prime contract must be done with care and attention to detail in order to both adequately protect the company and ensure that the services delivered are consistent with the terms of the prime contract.

6. <u>Insurance staff may not be aware of the contract requirements, or special liabilities and actions that must be taken for fulfilling insurance requirements under the prime contract.</u>

The insurance requirements imposed by the customer must be reviewed in detail by the company's insurance department. The company will have in place an existing insurance policy or policies, and these will limit at any time what insurance is available to the company. Standard insurance generally subscribed to by the company includes (1) Workers' Compensation and Employer's Liability,(2) Comprehensive General Liability Insurance (CGL) including Professional Liability, Blanket Contractual, Broad Form Property Damage, Completed Operations and Independent Contractor's Liability insurance, all applicable to Personal Injury, Bodily Injury and Property Damage and(3) Comprehensive Automobile Liability Insurance.

Where the A-E is performing a design-build contract, then a Builders All Risk Insurance (BAR) policy can be taken out and paid for by the customer as an extra premium charge under the contract. The Bar policy is a no fault insurance policy that protects the customer, and the company against the physical loss or damage to machinery, apparatus, materials, equipment, temporary forms, temporary structures, including contents and supplies used in the work being performed.

The company's standard insurance policies have finite dollar limits. The lowest possible insurance limits should be exposed in the contract. The company should then attempt to limit its indemnification liability under the contract to the risks insured and the actual amounts recovered under the insurances stated in the contract. This caps the company's liabilities, and exposes it to lower potential payouts under its policies. The company's insurance is a valuable asset, and needs to be protected to the maximum extent possible.

If the customer demands insurance coverage beyond the scope and limits of the company's policies then these can usually be procured but at additional cost to the customer.

When the customer desires that payment and performance bonds be procured, it is usually the responsibility of the insurance department to obtain the bond premium proposal, and the written terms of the bonds from the surety. These additional costs must be added to the proposed contract price at the time the proposal is submitted to the customer.

7. **The legal staff may not have reviewed the prime contract for special liability considerations, such as over reaching indemnification and warranty provisions that can expose the company to excessive liabilities and business threatening losses.**

Legal counsel should conduct a pre proposal review on every contract which contains out of policy provisions such as in the warranty (including performance guarantees of any type), indemnification, insurance, confidentiality and proprietary information, disclosures, patent and general liability areas.

Legal counsel should also be included in the review of every contract prior to the company signing the final contract.

One matter that deserves discussion here is indemnification. The customer seeks protection from damages and losses that arise during the company's performance of services under the contract. For this reason an indemnification clause in included in the contract.

The indemnification clause (an example of which is shown below in this section) normally promises the customer three things. The first is "indemnification" for any damages or losses suffered by the customer— this means out right payment by the company to or on behalf of the customer of any losses or damages which the customer may be forced to pay. The second is legal "defense" should the customer be sued by a third party on account of the performance of services. And the third protection is to be "held harmless" from any liabilities due to performance of the services.

These protections are of no value to the customer, however, unless the company has the financial capacity to follow through on them. That's a large reason why the insurance provided under the contract is important.

On the other hand the company seeks to limit its liability to the dollar limits and the types of insurances furnished under the contract. Furthermore, the company does not want to be liable under the indemnity for any portion of the damages or losses that are the result of customer negligence.

With these facts in mind the following is an indemnification clause that might be used in a contract:

"Company shall indemnify, defend and hold customer harmless, from and against liabilities, suits, loss, expense and damages for injury to or death of persons or damage to or destruction of property including, but not limited to, the property of customer, arising in connection with company's performance of the work and service pursuant to this Agreement except that caused by the

negligence of the customer or its contractors, agents or employees. Company's liability to the customer for all of the aforesaid matters is limited to the proceeds recovered from the insurance carried by company and within the coverage limits specified in the Insurance Article of this Agreement after settling claims of third parties."

In any event, the legal department should thoroughly review the indemnity clause offered by the customer and propose any desired changes to discuss with the customer during negotiations.

Another liability that must be protected against and limited arises from the company's warranty obligations under the contract. The company should obligate itself to perform its work to an industry recognized standard of care, and to limit its warranty obligation to remediation of any of its work that is not performed to that standard by performing (or re performing) any of its own services that have not been so performed. A warranty clause may read as follows:

Company warrants that the services rendered under this Agreement shall be performed in accordance with the standards customarily provided by an experienced and competent professional architect – engineering organization rendering the same or similar services. Company shall reperform any of said services which were not performed in accordance with this standard provided that Company is notified in writing by Customer of the nonconformity within 180 days after completion of the nonconforming service. Except as herein provided in respect of personal injury or property damage, the foregoing are Company's entire responsibilities and Customer's exclusive remedies for services rendered or to be rendered hereunder, and no other warranties, guarantees, liabilities or obligations are to be implied.

Finally, the company should seek an express exemption from consequential damages under the contract. Consequential Damages are those damages including indirect and special damages that result from the contract work and are reasonably foreseeable by the parties". A suggested consequential damages clause might read as follows:

In no event shall Company or its subcontractors or suppliers of any tier be liable in contract, tort, strict liability, warranty or otherwise, for any special, indirect, incidental or consequential damages, such as, but not limited to, loss of product, loss of anticipated profits or revenue, loss of use of the equipment or system, non-operation or increased expense of operation of other equipment or systems, cost of capital, or cost of purchased or replacement equipment or systems.

8. <u>Performing additional services without a formal change under the "changes" clause of the contract, thereby exposing the company to reduced profit, additional risks and schedule overruns.</u>

The contract should always contain a "Changes" clause. Under this clause the customer has the right to direct the company to perform changes in the work within the general scope of work of the contract. The company is obligated to perform the work as changed and to submit a claim for additional compensation, additional work and schedule adjustment. There is usually a time limit (e.g. 30 days) within which the claim for adjustment must be submitted to the customer.

The contract should always identify the customer representative who has the authority to direct changes under the 'changes' clause. This is someone separate from the customer's technical representative. Change order control must be enforced within the project to ensure that any new work which the customer directs is compensated for, and that any impacts to the statement of work and the schedule are negotiated, and incorporated into the contract.

The Project Manager (PM) or his designated person should be responsible for maintaining the change order log, and for pulling together the claim information, and following through to ensure that it is submitted within the deadline stated in the "changes" clause.

Whenever the customer's technical representative requests the company to perform additional services that should be authorized under the "changes" clause, the PM should promptly notify the technical representative of this fact in writing so that the parties can arrange for the necessary change order to be issued. Something that must be watched carefully, especially on fixed price, guaranteed maximum price, and cost plus fixed fee contracts is creeping work growth and costs under the contract. Under these types of contracts the company can particularly ill afford to neglect to have a disciplined change control approach to the project. Fixed price, GMP and fixed fee adjustments should be negotiated whenever new work is added and the "changes" clause should be implemented wherever deemed appropriate, and as often as necessary.

The following chapters are to acquaint the reader with the context and the nature of an approach to contract administration as it occurs in project based companies that is designed to avoid many of these pitfalls.

"Fixed Price, Guaranteed Maximum Price (GMP) and Cost- Plus- a-Fixed Fee(CPFF) adjustments should be negotiated wherever new work is added and the "changes" clause should be implemented wherever deemed appropriate and as often as necessary".

Contact administration, as a basic objective, ensures that the company is legally authorized to initiate and perform work. That the product/ service to be delivered is stated clearly in the contract. That the terms of payment are clear. That liabilities are controlled, capped and insured. And that the work is performed in compliance with the prime contract.

The employment of an experienced contract administrator (CA) is of extreme value.

In the A-E company the basic unit profit center is the individual customer funded project. Each project is directed by a project manager(PM).

Project sizes vary. A single report may be the only deliverable. Some projects are complex in which major facilities are to be designed and constructed.

An A-E company may be simple and small. One niche market may be the focus in which there are less than 100 employees. Or such companies may be complex and large where several markets are served, and hundreds, even thousands are employed.

The number of clients or customers served by the company is another variable. A company may focus on only a very few or a wide range of customers. This distinction will impact the complexity of the contract review/ administration requirements.

In a project driven company, regardless of size/complexity, <u>every project is authorized by a contract</u> which defines the work scope/statement, the schedule, compensation, liabilities, insurance, accounting and all other terms and conditions applicable to the project.

Effective contact administration will ensure that everyone in a staff discipline with input to the contract has had an opportunity to review and comment on the contract before the company signs it. These staff disciplines include, but are not limited to legal, tax, insurance, procurement and finance.

This Journal takes the reader through the project cycle, beginning with the pre-contact/proposal phase, through the performance phase. And finally the close-out phase of the project.

Chapter 2

Pre-contract, Proposal and Negotiation Phase

Contract administration begins in the proposal phase. The project must be reviewed for liability, insurance, tax and financial considerations before ever submitting a proposal.

In the pre-contract/proposal phase the company's management determines if the client's request for proposal (RFP) fits the company's business model and whether resources are available inside, and through possible subcontractors to perform the work. Management must also decide if the proposed work can be profitably performed under the terms and conditions, and other requirements, stated in the customer's Request for Proposal (RFP).

Potential competition must also be benchmarked to determine if other competitors may be in a superior position to win the project and, if so, whether the project may be better pursued as a joint venture or a specific prime/sub relationship, or not at all.

Assuming a proposed form of agreement is received with the RFP, it must be reviewed to determine that (1) the statement of work is clear, (2) the schedule is realistic,(3)there are no excessive liabilities or indemnifications, (4) insurance and tax considerations have been addressed, (5) the proper type of contact has been selected to fit the requirements of the proposed project (e.g. time and materials, fixed price, cost plus),(6) the terms and conditions provide for acceptable change and termination provisions, (7)subcontracting requirements are defined, and (8) the compensation, payment and audit terms are clear and acceptable.

Assuming that the company decides to proceed with the proposal, assignments are made to prepare and submit the necessary inputs to the designated PM.

The assigned Contract Administrator (CA) will provide comments on the proposed contract. These comments should provide an analysis of any risk elements that are part of the client's proposed contract agreement. And include contract review comments from legal, finance, tax, insurance, procurement and any other staff disciplines that have reviewed the contract.

The objective should be that the company gets to the negotiating table, and that the contract changes that are desired can be negotiated at that time. A phrase that can often be included in the proposal that will leave the contract open to negotiation is *"Any contract resulting from this proposal shall be subject to mutually acceptable terms and conditions."*

A negotiating team is assembled, assuming the company is selected for negotiations. This team is often headed up by a business development representative or PM who serves as the principal spokesperson for the contractor.

If there are contract terms/conditions to be resolved it is recommended that a CA be part of the team. This allows the negotiating team leader to distance himself from discussions over contract terms, often requiring extended debate.

Once negotiations have been completed the final agreement is prepared, usually by the customer. Sometimes, however, the company will do this where the customer is relying on the company for contracts expertise.

A negotiation memorandum details the final results of negotiations. The CA (or other designated person) may prepare this. It is approved by the negotiation team leader and forwarded to the customer as a record of key agreements reached in negotiations. This document may become important during contract performance. It interprets the intent of the parties. Can help resolve disputes and serve as a useful document in reviewing the final contract prior to signing.

Chapter 3

Contract Review and Execution Phase

The client will typically send the contract to the company for execution following the completion of negotiations. For compliance with agreements reached during negotiations the contract must be reviewed, as appropriate, by the necessary staff disciplines (finance, legal, tax, insurance), the CA and PM.

The CA prepares a transmittal memo to accompany the proposed contract through the <u>internal review process</u>. In essence, the transmittal memo that accompanies the contract through the internal review process is largely a <u>risk assessment memo</u> that informs management of any unusual terms and conditions or other provisions, including liability exposures that may accompany the performance of the contract.

The risk assessment memo and the accompanying agreement are reviewed and approved by the PM, the appropriate staff disciplines, business development, and when all concur, the contract is executed by the appropriate company manager, and returned to the customer for execution.

Where inconsistencies are found between the agreement as received by the company, and the terms that were agreed to during negotiations, these must be reconciled with the customer by the designated company representative.

Chapter 4

Project Initiation Phase

The project is normally initiated by receipt of the fully executed agreement from the client. Copies of the fully executed agreement should be provided as a minimum to the PM, and the staff discipline heads (legal, tax, finance, insurance, human resources).

Another method is for the client to expedite the initiation of work by issuing an NTP. An NTP requires that there be conditions within it that incorporate (by reference if necessary) the substance of the conditions that the parties plan to incorporate in the fully executed contract.

The NTP normally includes limitations as to (1) the duration of its effectiveness and (2) a maximum dollar amount above which the customer shall not be obligated to pay the company.

When the fully executed contract (or the NTP) is received by the company, a copy is immediately given to the finance and accounting department which is instructed to open a prime job and charge numbers in accordance with the work breakdown structure developed by the PM.

A work mobilization meeting should be held by the PM to inform the key personnel and staff discipline representatives that authorization to start work has been received and to provide instructions for commencing work.

Assuming that there is an assigned CA, he or she should prepare and distribute a digest of the pertinent contract provisions to all key project personnel and staff discipline heads.

This digest is known as a Contract Administration Summary (CAS). It generally contains the following contract provisions and instructions: name and address of the client, scope/statement of work, compensation and payment terms, billing instructions, period of performance, schedule of deliverables and milestones, special liability terms, subcontracting instructions, insurance requirements, changes clause, termination provisions, special client approval requirements, and any other terms of the contract that are essential to contract compliance in the daily performance of the project.

The CAS is intended as a guide to simplify the task of knowing the key contract provisions. This avoids the need for everyone involved in the project to read and be an expert on the entire agreement. The CAS should include the comment that a copy of the contract is on file with the CA. And that any help needed interpreting a particular provision of the contract can be provided by the CA.

During the project initiation phase the PM requests the CA to be responsible for interfacing with the staff discipline departments in the performance of their project startup responsibilities.

An important step in the project initiation phase is the establishment of the contract administration filing system.

Effective contract administration requires that all documents, both internal and external, be located in a filing system that ensures quick retrievability.

Contact administration files in the filing system suggested as a minimum are: Proposal; Precontract Correspondence; Negotiation Reports; Contract and Amendments; Contract Administration Summaries(CAS);

External Correspondence(non client); Client Correspondence; Internal Memos; Project Technical; Contract Progress Reports; Procurement/ Subcontracts; Change Orders/Change Order Proposals; Legal; Finance/ Accounting; Insurance; Tax; Human Resources; Contract Closeout.

Chapter 5

Project Performance Phase

To ensure that contract compliance is achieved throughout the term of the project is the main objective of contract administration. This requires that a checklist be developed of the stated contract requirements, and that these actually be checked off as completed.

As an example, certificates of insurance are generally to be provided within a stated number of days following the effective date of the contract. Monthly progress reports are required within a stated number of days following the end of the reporting period. Notifications to the client of reaching certain expenditure points are required. Client or customer written approvals to enter into subcontracts are usually necessary. Milestone dates are scheduled.

Contract administration requires that all of these agreement requirements be known, tracked and fulfilled.

The "changes" clause of the contract allows the customer to make, in most cases, unilateral changes in the services. The changes clause often requires that a claim for price adjustment be submitted within so many days (usually 30) following receipt of the change. The claim must address any impacts on the services, contract price, and schedule.

Sometimes the client or customer will attempt to include new work in the contract without going through the change order process. Effective contract administration "catches" these instances, and notifies the client in writing that these alterations are considered "changes" within the meaning of the changes clause, and that a claim for compensation, work and schedule adjustment will be submitted in accordance with the "changes" clause. This way the project remains under control, and appropriate work, compensation and schedule adjustments are documented and can be negotiated.

In this regard, the customer usually authorizes a single person to make changes in the contract. Accordingly, no work that the company considers to be a "change" should be performed unless authorized by the appropriate customer designated representative.

The CA, to do an effective job, needs to be included in project meetings involving contractual matters, and to work in close proximity with the PM to the maximum extent possible. The PM should use the CA to perform or coordinate contract compliance activities wherever possible. This takes the burden off the PM for these activities and places them on the CA.

Chapter 6

Project Closeout Phase

Following completion of the services, or delivery of the final deliverable the project closeout phase begins. A checklist of closeout actions may be taken directly from the contract. A Project Closeout Memo is prepared and issued by the CA to all key project personnel which describes the closeout actions to be taken, and by whom. For example, a final invoice must be prepared, and final payment received. This may take some time since all final billable costs must be in the billing system. A final release of claims may be required by the customer. Property borrowed and used by the company during the project may have to be returned. In addition there are internal requirements that must be fulfilled upon completion of the project. For example, job numbers have to be closed. Project personnel must be transferred to other projects. Internal facilities must be returned and redeployed elsewhere in the company. Staff disciplines must be notified of project completion so that they may complete their portions of the closeout, subcontracts must be closed out and final payments made to subcontractors, and final releases obtained. Project files must be sent to storage.

The project closeout phase is an important phase of the contract and must be correctly performed to ensure that all contractual and payment details have been finalized.

Chapter 7

Summary and Conclusion

Effective contract administration is vital to avoiding common pitfalls in the performance of projects. As such, sound contract administration increases the quality of performance, enhances the chances of securing repeat business, improves the organization's reputation in the industry, helps avoid costly mistakes, increases the likelihood that changes will be incorporated into the contract, increases the overall level of awareness of the organization in its project activities, allows project and company management to focus on important tasks that have a higher value to the overall performance of the organization, decreases the hidden costs of project performance and increases bottom line performance. For these reasons, the implementation of a disciplined approach to contract administration as has been described is in the company's best interests. The employment of experienced contract administrators is an important step in the advancement of this contract administration system.

Notes

Notes